cattus

The World of Cats

All inquiries should be addressed to:
Barron's Educational Series, Inc.
250 Wireless Boulevard
Hauppauge, New York 11788
http://www.barronseduc.com

Library of Congress Catalog Card No.: 99-26997

International Standard Book No. 0-7641-5210-6

Library of Congress Cataloging-in-Publication Data
Salviati, Stefano.
 [Univers du chat. English]
 The world of cats / Stefano Salviati ; photographs by Yves Lanceau.
   p.   cm.
 Includes bibliographical references (p.   ) and index.
 ISBN 0-7641-5210-6
 1. Cats. I. Title.
SF442.S3413   1999
636.8—dc21   99-26997
                                                 CIP

PRINTED IN SPAIN

9 8 7 6 5 4 3 2 1

The World of Cats

Text: Stefano Salviati

Photographs: Yves Lanceau

BARRON'S

Contents

Feline History

Bast,
the Cat-Goddess of Egypt

The remains of sacred cats were protected by a sarcophagus (wood, Roman era).

I f the cat had had a different fate in Egypt, its destiny throughout history would probably have been more modest. But the Egyptians elevated the cat to the ranks of the gods, and the renown of the small domestic cat, which originated in the East, spread first throughout the Greco-Roman world, then throughout the West. The cat's eye, capable of staring at the sun but still able to see in the shadows, profoundly disturbed the religious spirit of the Egyptian priests. They made the cat an androgynous deity, of both the sun and the moon.

The Egyptian cat, the *Felis silvestris libyca*, originated in the desert areas of Libya. It had already been domesticated 2,000 years before the modern era, as evidenced by the frescoes in Theban tombs, where the animal can be seen participating in the daily life of noble families. The appear-

A goddess in the form of a cat: Only recently domesticated, cats would carve out an impressive career in the Egypt of 4,000 years ago.

ance of the cat in Egypt is recounted in a mythological text, the Myth of the Eye of the Sun (c. 1500 B.C.): The lion goddess Sekhmet, sent to earth by her father, the Sun god Ra, to put down revolts, provoked wars and epidemics instead, then fled into the Nubian desert. Thot, the scribe of the gods, set out to find her, to reason with her, and it was with the calm features of the cat-goddess Bast that Sekhmet reappeared. This legend is likely confirmation of the disappearance of the lion from Egypt, followed by the proliferation of the cat throughout the country. A useful animal, endowed with the ability to eliminate rats and mice, scorpions and snakes, the cat quickly became a companion with whom the Egyptians shared their daily lives, but also and above all, a god. In its male incarnation, it is the "Great Cat" of Heliopolis, the protector

Bast was sometimes shown stretched out, playing with one or several kittens (bronze, Ptolemaic era).

A painted cloth mask make[s] it possible to identify the features of a mummified cat (Late era).

This bronze statuette (Late era) shows the goddess Bast as a woman with the head of a cat carrying a sistrum, whose sound frightens demons, the willow basket of the midwife, and the eye of Oudjat to ensure health. The cult of Bast attracted large crowds to the Bubastis temple during the Nile flooding season.

of the sleeping god Ra, sailing each night on his small boat in the kingdom of the dead, suddenly brandishing a knife in his paw to stab the snake, Apophis, who is attempting to hinder Ra in his voyage. Thanks to the "Great Tomcat," the sun rises each day at dawn, and the balance of the universe is preserved.

The female incarnation of the sacred cat is Bast, goddess of maternity, protector of pregnant women and the newborn, patron of doctors, wise men, and midwives, goddess of music and dance. Bast is usually represented either in the form of a sitting cat, wearing on its chest the powerful talisman of the eye of Oudjat, or in the form of a woman with the head of a cat holding a sistrum, a musical instrument consecrated to her, along with the willow basket of a midwife. The temple of Bast stood in Bubastis, in the Nile delta. By the end of the dynastic period, before the Roman conquest, the cat-goddess had become the most popular of the Egyptian deities.

In this fresco from a tomb in the Valley of the Nobles (Luxor), the cat appears in its role as predator of birds, in the middle of a swamp.

Could the Egyptian Mau have served as the model for this elegant statuette of Bast?

A Guardian Spirit

A tiger cat seizes a chicken in a mosaic from Pompeii.

Herodotus, traveling in Egypt approximately 500 years before the modern era, introduced the cat to his Greek countrymen, who lost no time in stealing specimens from the land of the Pharaohs when they were not purchasing them from the Phoenician merchants who sold them commercially. Replacing the weasel as the predator of rodents, the cat was appreciated by the Greeks and later by the Romans for its beauty. Mosaics, pottery, and stelae provide evidence of the establishment of the domestic cat in the Greco-Roman world. The animal would play another role there, inherited from Egypt: Assimilated into the ranks of the household gods, as guardian spirit, it accompanied deceased children as they entered the great beyond. The cat, enshrined in Rome in a temple dedicated to Liberty, was a favorite animal of the Roman legions. It was probably during the invasion of Gaul that the domestic cat, a native of the East, made its discrete but certain entrance.

The Cat at the Stake

Louis XV had to put an end to the tradition of the fires of Midsummer's Eve, in Paris. His predecessors did not hesitate to give the signal initiating the massacre of cats.

The Christian West quickly came to consider the cat as an enemy. While it was unknown at the time that the animal came from the East, it was considered to be the companion of witches who, for the most part, were the last priestesses of the lunar cults of Egypt and Rome. After the Council of Tours (567) prohibited sacrifices to the dead and other surviving pagan rites, cats and witches became targets of the Church's intolerance. Expiatory fires would be lit. The fear that the world would end in the year 1000, the Black Death that invaded Europe with the return of Crusaders, and famine created a climate of fear: The cat contributed, in spite of itself, to exorcising this terror. Because it was the companion of witches, accompanying them to the sabbath, it would also be consigned to the flames. Throughout Europe, on certain religious holidays, such as the first Sunday of Lent, Midsummer's Eve, or Halloween, cats were burned at the stake. The most notorious of these rites took place in Paris, at the Place de Grève, on Midsummer's Eve. The King of France, himself, came to light the bonfire that would consume a full sackload of cats. To the delight of the crowd, he persuaded that, in this way, the devil was held in check.

Pilgrims' Passage

Prior to the arrival of the Europeans, there were no known indigenous domestic cats in America, and no one knows for sure how or when the first ones got here. Perhaps the Vikings, Columbus, or other foreign travelers brought a litter ashore, as it was common practice in those days to take cats on long sea voyages to hunt the rats and mice that devoured the ship's food supplies. Because cats appear in early American art, we know that they arrived here by the 1600s or so, which suggests that they sailed across the Atlantic with the European colonists. As a result, North America's domestic cats are believed to be descendants of cats brought from the British Isles and other western European countries.

Once ashore, the seafaring felines were let loose to continue their rodent control duties in the fields and barns of America's pioneers. For centuries, these working mousers flourished as natural selection molded them into a lot as hardy and durable as the settlers among whom they lived.

By the late 1800s, people began to view cats as more than mere mousers. After Harrison Weir held the first cat show in London, England, in 1871, it didn't take long for interest in such events to reach American shores. Since that time, cat exhibitions have taken place in the United States, but an official all-breed show held in 1895 at New York's Madison Square Garden marked the real beginning of the North American cat fancy. In 1899, the American Cat Association (ACA), the oldest U.S. cat registry and the first of many, was formed to keep records of show wins and pedigrees.

As cat shows and the *cat fancy*—the collective term for the business of breeding and showing purebred cats—gained in popularity in America, so did the idea of keeping cats as companions. People even began importing exotic breeds, such as the pointed Siamese as well as the longhaired Persian and Angora types, from abroad. These cats mingled with the domestic shorthairs already on native soil, thus leading to America's diversity of domestic cats.

The Flemish painter Otto Van Veen—or Otto Venius—
(1556–1629) is shown surrounded by his family and
his cat in this 1584 painting.

The fashion for longhair cats, Angora or Persian, is shown in
this painting by O. Le Roy entitled Collar of Honor.

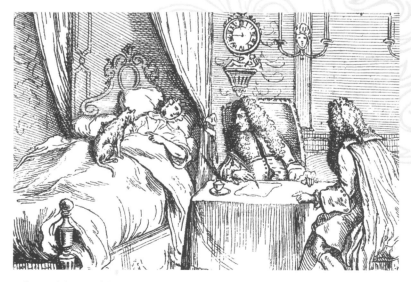

The celebrated harpist Mademoiselle Dupuy drawing up her
will in favor of her cat. Engraving by Charles Coypel
appearing in Moncrif's Cats (1727).

Artists' Companion

That which disturbed man in the Middle Ages fascinated and inspired him in the Romantic Era: The diabolical eye of the cat became, under the pen of Charles Baudelaire, the "mystical eye." Hypersensitive, the cat was the incarnation of the ideal muse of a generation of poets and artists that viewed it as the ideal medium, the symbol of the creative imagination. From Leonardo da Vinci, who has been credited with declaring that "the smallest feline is a masterpiece," to the likes of T. S. Eliot and Mark Twain, many appreciated the animal's affectionate presence in their daily lives. While cat protection societies (such as the ASPCA, founded in 1866) made their debuts, a French journalist, Jules Husson, whose pen name was Champfleury, wrote the first major study of domestic cats, titled *Les Chats (Cats)*, in 1869. The book was illustrated by his artist friend, Edouard Manet. The era of the domestic cat arrived with the dawn of the twentieth century, as Moncrif predicted. While cats became the conquerors of more and more households, they invaded the screen, the musical theater, literature and comic strips, painting and advertising. Ethologists studied their behavior, doctors their positive influence on our well-being, and sociologists their status as social phenomenon. Now, at the end of the century, the *Felis silvestris catus* outnumbers, in our homes, its eternal rival, the dog. This is due to the fact that it is more adaptable to the constraints of urban life, and perhaps also because the cat, with the prestigious aura of its Egyptian origins, satisfies our imagination and our aesthetic sense at the same time as it fulfills our thirst for affection.

Praised by nineteenth-century poets, and specifically by Baudelaire, the cat became the symbol of the bohemian life of Montmartre and its provocatively inspired artists.

In 1882 Salis founded a poetic and literary review in the spirit of his cabaret, Le Chat Noir (The Black Cat). In 1922 Desbardieux created this poster to celebrate its reissue.

Parisian writers, poets, and talented artists gathered at the celebrated cabaret Le Chat Noir (The Black Cat), founded in 1881 by the wine merchant Rodolphe Salis. Toulouse-Lautrec, Alphonse Allais, and Yvette Guilbert were regular customers.

The popularity of the cat may be assessed thanks to the large number of works devoted to it since the end of the previous century. It was no longer a question of demonizing the animal: It had now become a friend.

Colette, who devoted many pages to cats, played her favorite animal, in 1912, on the Ba-Ta-Clan stage, in a pantomime, La Chatte Amoureuse (The Amorous Cat).

Longhair, Shorthair

Wild Cats

The forest cat resembles the domestic tiger cat, but its fur is much thicker.

The eye "make-up" of the wild cat always follows the same design, with a black band that extends the eye and a second that underlines it.

Long pursued and massacred, the forest cat of Europe, or wild cat —*Felis silvestris silvestris*—has today become rare. Its link with the domestic cat had long been a mystery. We now know that it originated in the East, as did our domestic cat, to whom it is closely related. It should not be confused with the feral cat, a domestic cat that has returned to live in the wild.

Legend has made the wild cat a terrifying animal, confused in the imagination with the wolf. The reality is quite different, as the forest cat is a timid animal that is afraid of man and keeps its distance from him. It tolerates cold well and lives by hunting. It is a predator of small rodents, much like the domestic cat. Present in deciduous forests throughout Europe, the wild cat, a protected species in France since 1979, can still be found in Lorraine, Burgundy, the Auvergne and in the Pyrenees.

In its forest habitat, the wild cat often takes refuge in trees in order to survey its territory.

Although it gives the impression of being much larger than the domestic cat, that is only because of its coat: A male weighs from 9 to 16 pounds (4.5 to 7.5 kg), and a female from 8 to 11 pounds (4 to 5 kg).

The wild cat moves around a lot. A male's territory can cover 740 to 990 acres (300 to 400 ha); females are more stable.

A magnificent animal, but even kittens are totally resistant to domestication.

In the forest, the wild cat makes its home in the stumps and trunks of trees, and even in the crevices of rocks.

On the back of the tiger coat is a black line that follows the spinal column, a characteristic of the wild breed.

The club tail, on which the black rings are clearly visible, is also typical of the wild cat.

Shorthair
Cats

These are the most numerous, with some 30 breeds originating in Europe, Asia, the Near East, and North America. For many cat fanciers, the uncrowned king is the ordinary or domestic cat, as cats are increasingly the world's most popular pets. In the United States, cats outnumber dogs in households by nearly two to one, probably because they are less demanding to care for than dogs. The ordinary shorthair cat retains its appeal because of its low maintenance care and grooming. The domestic cat's origins have long been a mystery, and it is now believed to be descended either from the ornate cat, which still exists in a wild state in Iran, Pakistan, and Afghanistan, or from the wild cat of Libya, which came from Egypt. Arriving in Europe via Greece and Rome, the domestic cat established itself in spite of the persecution to which it was subject in the Middle Ages.

BENGAL

A true apartment leopard, the Bengal is the result of a cross with an Asian wild cat.

AMERICAN CURL

With short or medium-long hair, the American Curl is distinguishable by its ears in the shape of a crescent moon.

RUSSIAN BLUE

Brought to England in the last century by Russian sailors, the Russian Blue originated in Archangel, on the shores of the White Sea.

AMERICAN SHORTHAIR

Its ancestors came from Europe to conquer America: The American Shorthair is the direct cousin of our domestic cat.

RUSSIAN BLUE

More slender than the Chartreux, the Russian Blue has a silver blue coat and magnificent emerald green eyes. With its strong personality, this cat is very close to its master, and seems rather exclusive and authoritarian.

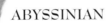

ABYSSINIAN

With a coat resembling that of a hare, the Abyssinian originated not in Ethiopia (formerly Abyssinia) or in Egypt, as was long believed, but in Southeast Asia, on the shores of the Indian Ocean.

BENGAL

From its wild origins, the Bengal has retained, despite appearances, a sturdy character.

AMERICAN WIREHAIR

The result of a spontaneous mutation, the American Wirehair has fur that is wavy, stiff, and curly.

ABYSSINIAN

The Abyssinian is distinguishable by its large almond eyes. The color of its coat and its ticking (alternating light and dark bands) becomes fixed only at the end of the first year.

Shorthair *Cats*

BOMBAY

A mini black panther, the Bombay is the result of a cross between a black American Shorthair and a sable Burmese.

Among the oldest breeds of shorthair cats, there are two that are distinguished by their silver blue coats: the Chartreux and the Russian Blue. The first may have originated in Turkey or Iran and been brought back to Europe by the Crusaders. In his *Epitaph for a Cat,* which he wrote for his cat Belaud (1558), Joachim Du Bellay confirms the presence of the Chartreux in France. Its name comes from the resemblance of its fur to a woolen fabric, the "pile des chartreux." Its popularity has been challenged by the British Blue. For its part, the Russian Blue, formerly known as the Maltese, and recognized in England since 1960, has experienced a spectacular revival, after nearly disappearing following the Second World War.

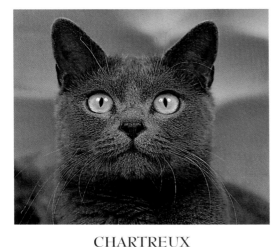

CHARTREUX

Its vibrant orange eyes distinguish it from the emerald green eyes of the Russian Blue.

JAPANESE BOBTAIL

The Japanese Bobtail is also distinguished by its shorter hind legs.

JAPANESE BOBTAIL

Called Mi-Ke in its own country, it has the reputation of bringing good luck. Its embryonic rolled tail is "in the shape of a chrysanthemum."

BURMILLA

When a chinchilla Persian meets a female lilac Burmese, that is the secret of the Burmilla!

BURMESE

Not to be confused with the Birman, the Burmese is an oriental cat originating, like the Siamese, in Southeast Asia. The points of the Burmese are subtly visible under the beautiful chocolate coat.

BRITISH SHORTHAIR

The British Shorthair exists in some 120 varieties including tabby, tortoiseshell, smoked, silver shaded, chinchilla, monocolored, and bicolored.

RUSSIAN BLUE

The Russian Blue has been called the "Archangel Blue" after the city of Archangel, from which it arrived in the last century, and its admirers claim that it has the ability to smile.

CALIFORNIA SPANGLED CAT

The product of a number of amazing crossings, the California Spangled Cat was born from a Hollywood screenwriter's desire to own a replica of an African wild cat.

BRITISH SHORTHAIR

Like the European, the British Shorthair is an improved version of the domestic cat. Here, the Persian has played a role in the crossing.

Shorthair
Cats

EUROPEAN SHORTHAIR

Whatever the variety, in this case golden tabby, it easily adapts to family life.

Why are Manx cats consistently born without tails? Legend has it that it is the fault of Noah, who closed the door of the ark too quickly . . . The reality, less brutal, is a spontaneous mutation documented for more than two centuries. The Egyptian Mau bears an uncanny resemblance to the cats represented in the tombs of the Valley of the Kings. A relative of the Abyssinian, this spotted tabby actually originated in the land of the pharaohs. The Oriental has its roots much further away, in Thailand. For a long time, it was neglected in favor of its close relative, the Siamese, with its color-pointed coat. The Korat and the Havana belong to the same Oriental family.

MANX

When its fur is of medium length, the Manx changes its name and is called Cymric, which means "Welsh."

MANX

The balance of this tailless cat does not seem disturbed by its strange physical characteristic.

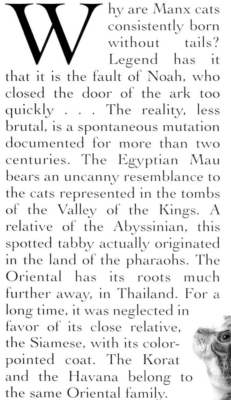

MANX

The Manx cat owes its somewhat bouncy gait to its raised hindquarters.

EGYPTIAN MAU

An unsettling resemblance with the painted face of Egyptian mummies.

EUROPEAN SHORTHAIR

European by name, but alley cat in its soul, this domestic cat remains true to form.

KORAT

Originating in Thailand, the Korat, with its silver blue coat and green eyes, resembles the Siamese as it was during the last century.

ORIENTAL SHORTHAIR

More than 90 varieties, from monocolor to silver spotted tabby, in a single breed: The Oriental is in no danger of disappointing its admirers.

HAVANA BROWN

The Havana Brown, a successful crossing of a chocolate Siamese and a black European.

ORIENTAL SHORTHAIR

Lively, elegant, very much a presence, and attached to its master, the Oriental is as "talkative" as its close relative, the Siamese.

OCICAT

Cross the Abyssinian and the Siamese and you will get the Ocicat, so named for its resemblance to the ocelot.

Shorthair Cats

CORNISH REX

The Rex owes its name to a rabbit with curly fur noted in France around 1919.

DEVON REX

A real bat cat, the Devon Rex accentuates its appearance with curly whiskers and eyelashes!

"Sacred cat! Royal cat! Cat of Siam!" This triple invocation from the pen of Colette describes the prestige of a breed documented since the fourteenth century in its native country and whose European beginnings were eventful: The first specimens of the Siamese introduced in France in 1885 were considered to be so bizarre that they found a place in the zoo at the Jardin des Plantes! A sacred animal in what later became Thailand, the Siamese must have been an excellent temple guardian, with its strong, resonant voice sounding the alarm. Today, along with the Persian, it is justifiably the most widely celebrated breed.

The British Isles seem to prefer spontaneous mutations. The Scottish Fold, with its folded ears, appeared in 1961. The Rex, with its curly coat and long ears, appeared around 1950 in Cornwall and a decade later in Devon, then made its appearance in the United States.

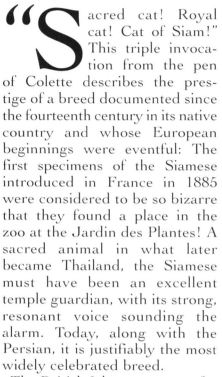

SIAMESE

Siamese admirers love it with an unusually long muzzle, or with one that is more modest.

TONKINESE

A cross between a Siamese and a Burmese, the Tonkinese is a cat that is rarely seen in Europe.

DEVON REX

SIAMESE

The Siamese is the uncontested favorite of anyone who appreciates an extremely lively cat. Always in motion, and in constant conversation with the Eternal, the Siamese is very engaging, and is very attached to its master.

SCOTTISH FOLD

With its ears folded forward, the Scottish Fold seems to be wearing a cap.

SELKIRK REX

The most recent member of the Rex clan, the Selkirk appeared in the United States in 1987.

SCOTTISH FOLD

Blessed with an amiable personality, the Scottish Fold is a cat that adapts easily to apartment life, where it enjoys spending peaceful days.

SELKIRK REX

Contrary to its British "cousins," the Selkirk Rex does not have enormous ears. Only about 50 of these specimens exist.

SCOTTISH FOLD

The Scottish Fold is a rarity, as the mutation affecting its ears often causes skeletal deformities.

SINGAPURA

Discovered, as its name indicates, on the island of Singapore, this very small cat with enormous eyes first charmed Americans prior to making itself known in Europe.

Medium-hair Cats

NORWEGIAN FOREST CAT

The Vikings brought this majestic cat from the Caspian Sea to Scandinavia, where it was known as the Skogkatt.

Why does nature endow some cats with fur that is longer than that of a shorthair, but not as long as that of the Persian? Genetics provides the answer: A mutant recessive gene is responsible.

There are hardly more than one dozen breeds of medium-hair cats. There are European types, like the Norwegian Forest Cat, the Birman, the Turkish Angora, and the Turkish Van, Persian types like the Exotic Shorthair, and Oriental types, like the Balinese, the Somali, the Javanese, and the Tiffany. There is a legend surrounding the Birman, whose ancestors guarded the temple of the goddess Tsun Kyan Tse. The Birmans' sky-blue eye color was given to them because of the courage they displayed defending their companions, the priests. In reality, the Birman appeared in France around 1923, the result of a cross between a Siamese and a longhair cat. But doesn't such a beautiful cat deserve to have such a legendary past?

MAINE COON

Legend has it that the Maine Coon is the product of an amorous encounter between a feral cat and a raccoon!

BIRMAN

The colored points of the Birman develop their intensity only after two or three years.

NORWEGIAN FOREST CAT

Is there any need to note that this vigorous and athletic cat is more at ease in a garden than confined to the house?

BALINESE

The Balinese (along with its close relative the Javanese) is in fact a medium-hair Siamese. Moreover, it exhibits the same behavior as the Siamese, and has the same stentorian voice!

MAINE COON

This American giant can weigh up to 19 pounds (9 kg) and is perhaps the result of a spontaneous mutation of the American Shorthair.

SOMALI

The Somali is one of nature's marvels. Its mottled coat and its appearance indicate its kinship with the Abyssinian. However, it is considered to be a completely separate breed.

RAGDOLL

A relative of the Birman, the Ragdoll is a real charmer.

EXOTIC SHORTHAIR

A real little bear, the Exotic Shorthair resembles both its parents, the American Shorthair and the Persian.

Longhair Cats

TURKISH VAN

Among the major assets of the Turkish Van are its magnificent eyes, amber or blue in color. Many specimens have eyes of different colors, one amber and the other blue. This characteristic is much sought-after by cat fanciers.

How can we speak of longhair cats without paying tribute to the mythical Angora, today almost completely supplanted by the Persian, but to whom the latter perhaps owes its sumptuous coat? Known in Europe since the seventeenth century, the Angora has so marked our feline culture that many people tend to call any longhair cat an "angora." The Turkish Angora, a native of the high plateaus of Anatolia and Iran, was long considered in its home country as a sort of living jewel, worthy of being given as a gift for its beauty, as one would give a precious gem. In his *Natural History,*

Mandarin

Burron names it as one of the four breeds of cats known in the eighteenth century. Unfortunately, the Turkish Angora then suffered a less enviable fate. In its native country, it left the palaces to evolve in the streets, and the breed seemed destined to become extinct. In other countries, it was supplanted by the Persian in the hearts of cat fanciers. The persistence of certain breeders made it possible to save this worthy representative of one of the most illustrious breeds in the natural world. The same was true for its cousin, the Turkish Van, living in the high plateaus of Kurdish territory. In its native land, less than 100 specimens of this swimming cat survived, and the species might have vanished entirely without the efforts of local zoologists and a handful of committed breeders, both in Europe and the United States.

TURKISH VAN

The Turkish Van, sometimes classified as a medium-hair cat, has a unique personality. It attaches itself to its owner so completely that it can die in his or her absence. It does not tolerate the presence of other cat breeds very well.

TURKISH ANGORA

More slender and more delicate than the Turkish Van, the Turkish Angora had a great deal of difficulty in establishing itself in the world of professional cat breeding, some individuals mistakenly considering it to be a variety of domestic cat.

TURKISH VAN

Even far from the lakes where its ancestors were born, the Turkish Van remains an aquatic cat. It has even been known to join its master in the bathtub!

MANDARIN

Mastery of the laws of genetics has made it possible to create longhair varieties of some shorthair breeds: here, a Mandarin Oriental Blue Tabby, its silky fur enhanced by dark stripes.

TURKISH ANGORA

Is he dreaming of his native land?

Longhair Cats

TORTOISESHELL PERSIAN

Among the parti-colored Persians, the tortoiseshell, with its topaz eyes, is much sought-after.

A direct descendant of the Angora, the Persian is without doubt the most spectacular of cats, and perhaps the most popular, if we are to judge by its imposing presence in cat shows. Its name was selected rather arbitrarily, the Angoras from which it is descended having lived within Turkey and the former Persia. The Persian cats that we admire today have little in common with the first specimens that arrived in Italy in the seventeenth century. They are the result of patient work by British breeders since the end of the nineteenth century. The breed today boasts an astonishing number of colors and varieties: There are more than 100 of them!

TRICOLOR PERSIAN

An ornamental cat, the Persian appreciates a calm apartment existence.

CHINCHILLA PERSIAN

Of all the varieties, the Chinchilla Persian can boast of always having been the favorite of advertisers.

BLUE CREAM PERSIAN

A combination of blue and rust, the Blue Cream is a recent creation.

COLORPOINT PERSIAN

BICOLOR PERSIAN

The Bicolor Persian combines white with an infinite number of shades: blue, black, chocolate, lilac, red, and cream. This coloring must form an inverted V on the forehead.

COLORPOINT PERSIAN

With the wink of an eye to the Siamese, Colorpoint Persians make it possible to see, under their abundant fur, the face and the various markings of the cat from Siam.

TORTOISESHELL PERSIAN

Flat nose like a Pekinese or straight? Each has its admirers.

Kittens

SCOTTISH FOLD

These Scottish Fold kittens, demonstrating a kind of poise, already have the "cap-like" folded ears that distinguish their breed.

MAINE COON

These small Maine Coon cats will get big. This "wild" cat, born in the United States, reaches an impressive weight: 17 to 22 pounds (8 to 10 kg) for males, 15 to 15 pounds (6 to 7 kg) for females.

C hildhood, for cats, lasts only a few short months, since a cat reaches maturity in less than one year. Anyone who loves cats especially cherishes a litter of kittens that can be tirelessly observed. Delightful in their clumsiness, which is quickly outgrown, then agile, lively, mischievous, continually hungry, and curious about new experiences, kittens learn very quickly from their mothers how to groom themselves and to hunt. Sleeping and nursing occupy a good portion of their days. Then comes playtime, a comical show for us, but educational for these future predators who, in this way, learn how to feed and defend themselves.

The kitten becomes socialized between the second and seventh week of life: it is imperative that it come in contact with humans and be handled by a variety of people, or else it will remain timid and difficult to domesticate. What the kitten learns during this period remains engraved in its memory.

CREAM BRITISH SHORTHAIR

Kittens begin to see properly after one to two weeks.

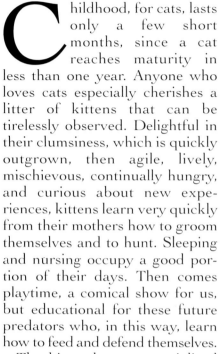

BRITISH SHORTHAIR

This British Shorthair is demonstrating a perfect "on guard" posture that is one of the basic figures in feline play.

NORWEGIAN FOREST CAT

The art and manner of feigning innocence between two rounds of devilish play . . .

A COMPANION

A special bond develops between cat and child, and the child can tell the cat everything.

RAGDOLL

These ragdoll kittens, that seem doubled up with laughter, demonstrate how easy it is to attribute human characteristics to the cat.

DEVON REX

Is this a little lamb with bat's ears? Not at all: The Devon Rex has a wavy coat, enormous eyes, and equally large ears that give it its unique look.

COLORPOINT PERSIAN

This Colorpoint Persian is setting out on tiptoes to discover the world.

Rare Cats

SPHINX

Very curious by nature, the Sphinx is a very possessive cat that attaches itself to its master and has an affectionate, loving, and even clinging personality!

Spontaneous mutations or the result of selective breeding, new cats occasionally make their appearance, for better or for worse! Unusual is the term used to describe these rare breeds of cat whose aesthetic appeal is sometimes doubtful.

The most famous of all is undoubtedly the Sphinx, or naked cat, which appeared for the first time following a natural mutation experienced by a common Canadian cat in 1966. While it does not have fur, its bicolored skin is covered with a very fine down that feels like suede to the touch.

Born in Germany in 1987 from the crossbreeding of a Scottish Fold and a Rex, the Pudelkatze, or poodle cat, has the folded ears of the former and the curly fur of the latter. The Munchkin Cat was born in the United States in 1994, the result of a natural mutation. Its compatriot, the Pixie Bob, is probably the result of an amorous encounter between a female domestic cat and a small wild cat.

SPHINX

Reproduction of the Sphinx is difficult, with the majority of kittens dying at birth. The young Sphinx has light fur on the back, which quickly disappears.

SPHINX

The absence of fur does not make the Sphinx susceptible to cold. In the winter, it develops a layer of fat under the skin, which gives this specimen a wrinkled appearance. Nevertheless, this cat must live indoors.

MUNCHKIN CAT

PIXIE BOB

Presented for the first time in France in 1998, the Pixie Bob is occasionally born without a tail, like the Manx and the Japanese Bobtail.

MUNCHKIN CAT

This doesn't only happen to dogs! The cat, also, can be afflicted with "bassetism," as illustrated by the Munchkin Cat. American breeders are very proud of these "hedgehoppers." Are they right or wrong?

SPHINX

Could this be a close relative of E.T., the extraterrestrial?

SPHINX

The Sphinx is a particularly playful and mischievous cat.

Street Cats

A melancholy look: Was this street cat perhaps abandoned?

They used to be called stray cats; the term "free cats" that is now being given them has certainly restored a portion of their dignity. "I am the cat who goes out alone, and everyplace is home," said the solitary hero of the famous story by Rudyard Kipling. Times change, and so do ways of thinking. The creation in the last century of the first major associations for the protection of animals, such as the ASPCA, made it possible for street cats to see themselves accepted, little by little, in the urban and rural environments where they survive as best they can.

These cat populations are found in the most unusual places: cemeteries, public and private gardens, courtyards and basements of old houses, parking garages, warehouses. Anywhere it is possible to find shelter, cats will take refuge, in groups of various sizes.

Their friends? Protectors and friends of cats, each of whom looks after a colony to which they are attached, passing by each day—or even at night, in order

Is it nap time?

Street cat or not, it's good to keep in practice.

Lounging in the sun, an inalienable right.

Dinner must be found on your own . . .

Resourcefulness above all: survival requires it.

not to attract attention—to distribute food to the hungry ones anxiously awaiting their arrival. With the help of associations, protectors work to tattoo and sterilize the street cats who, maintained in their natural environment, contribute in their own way to the ecological balance of cities. The quintessential city of cats, Venice has understood this. Here, cats, protected and monitored, participate in the well-being of the residents by keeping down the number of rodents. The presence of cats, which adds to the aesthetic beauty of Venice, is greatly appreciated by tourists.

Waiting together for a friend to bring food makes the wait seem shorter.

While street cats also have enemies, their status is improving in most of the great European cities. In Paris, Rome, Amsterdam, and London, numerous efforts have been made so that cats without a home can one day hope to live without fear. Perhaps there would be fewer homeless cats if those who adopt them would be more responsible by not abandoning them when they are no longer found to be "amusing"!

All of the pride of the cat can be seen in this vigilant male.

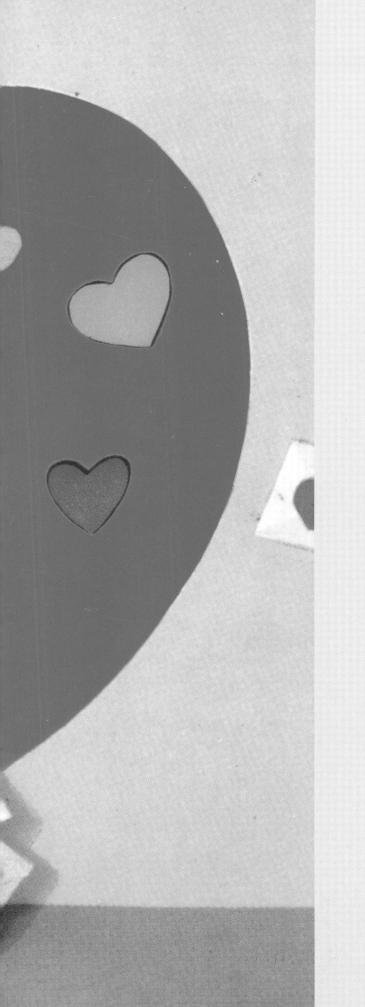

The Words to Say It

Meow

"I call a cat a cat, and Rollet a rascal." Thus literature established, for posterity, by way of a satire by Boileau, the name that we all know. But the word "cat" was not pulled out of a magician's hat. The word "chat" appeared in French in 1175, preceding by several decades the feminine form of the word (chatte), in anticipation of the word "chaton" (kitten), which was officially born in 1261. The term *felis*, which means cat in Latin (and which is found in the generic term "feline") was lost along the way, replaced by the term *cattus* from the low Latin, beginning in the fourth century; our word "cat" is the direct descendent. This semantic evolution is most likely proof of the influx of cats from Egypt and North Africa to Rome at that time: *cattus*, similar to the Arabic *(qitt)*, Berber *(qott)*, and Syrian *(kadista)* words for cat took the place of *felis*. Everyone knows that cats, in mewing, emit a sound similar to meow: an onomatopoeia that came later.

Milk

The image of the cat lapping its milk from a bowl is so deeply anchored in our minds that the first gesture that we make, if by chance we should come across an abandoned cat, is to offer it some milk. There is certainly a kind of affection in connection with this vital liquid that nourishes both the human child and the kitten. Eroticism is also an element here, as witnessed by the famous song by Georges Brassens in which "all the guys in the village" gather around to see the good Margot "open her blouse to suckle her cat"! We know, from the Greek historian Diodorus of Sicily, that the sacred cats from the temple of Bubastis, in Egypt, were fed with bread soaked in milk—in times past, the traditional meal for the country cat. However, although the cat likes it, milk is often poorly tolerated; cats often have difficulty digesting the lactose that causes diarrhea. Milk should be consumed in moderation!

The kitten's first nourishment is colostrum, secreted before milk from the mother's teats in the hours immediately following delivery. This liquid immunizes the newborn kittens against disease for several weeks.

Purring

Purring is perhaps the feline method of communication that speaks directly to our hearts. What is more tender, more calming, than a cat purring in our arms while we pet it? It used to be said that the purring cat was "turning its spinning wheel," so regular is the animal's breathing during this activity. We interpret the purring of the cat as a sign of contentment: It willingly purrs to greet us, when we give it food, and when we pet it—all agreeable situations. In fact, this idea must be broadened to that of communication. Kittens purr when they suckle at the teats of their mother, who responds in kind. By purring, the cat opens a dialogue with us on matters it considers important, whether pleasant or not. Thus it is possible to hear a sick cat, or one in agony, purring. A cat giving birth does the same. A cat experiencing fear or anxiety will also purr, at the veterinarian's office, for example. . . . For a long time, purring was a mystery for scientists. It was not known by what mechanism the cat, when inhaling and exhaling, could emit this sound that is so specific to certain felines. The phenomenon takes place high in the muscles of the larynx and the glottis, and it is aerodynamic. In addition to purring, the cat has several other means of vocal expression: meowing, trilling, growling, and crying.

Each vocalization has its meaning, and in this way the animal can make itself understood both to other cats and to its master. Whether it is expressing a call, a request, astonishment, contentment, pain, fear, sexual desire, menace, among other things, the adult cat has its own "vocabulary" supported by some 15 different vocalizations, which make it an animal well equipped for communication.

Fish

"Cats love fish, but they hate to get their paws wet." This proverb, well known in France, England, and Italy, promotes the presumed laziness of the cat, but indicates a superficial knowledge of the animal's behavior. Nature has made it possible for the cat to be able to seize a fish, a food of which it is particularly fond, if the occasion presents itself. All it has to do is use one of its forepaws like a spoon, a gesture that it has mastered thanks to the hunting games it has played since kittenhood.

If prey is available in a pond or stream, it is not unusual for a cat, ignoring its presumed dislike of water, to plunge in its paw to try to catch it. Here, the Turkish Van is a veritable phenomenon, swimming to perfection and diving to bring up the fish, which it will then consume on the shore. Nevertheless, it is better to give your cats cooked fish.

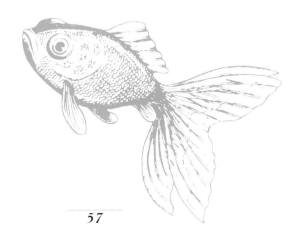

A superb hunter, the cat can spend a long time lying in wait for its prey.

Mice

Mice, rats, field mice. If they did not exist, the cat would certainly not have played the same role for our ancestors, and would probably have remained a half-wild animal! It is as a predator that the people of antiquity most appreciated the cat, before discovering that it could also be a pleasant companion in daily life. We understand why the Greeks and the Romans, captivated by Herodotus's tales of travel in Egypt, approximately 500 B.C., and his accounts of feline adventures, wanted to possess these animals unknown to them. To combat rodents they had only weasels and snakes, species that were hardly compatible with domestic life. The cat appears cruel—to our eyes—when it plays with the mouse it is about to kill. Its simple presence and its surrounding odor are generally enough to discourage rodents from entering a cat's territory and meeting an unenviable end!

Our sensitivities, as animal lovers, are often shocked by what we consider the cruelty of the cat. Even domesticated and fed, the cat remains a predator.

Raised with a mouse since birth, a kitten will later do it no harm.

Femininity

Poets have often praised the feline grace of their feminine muses. Look for the woman, and it is often the elegant kitty to which you will find her compared. Is there similarity in the beauty of their bearing, charm, and perhaps also in their changeable—and often cunning—personalities? If we look back in history, we see that this relationship between woman and cat is among one of the most prestigious. The great Egyptian goddesses, Nout, Isis, and Bast, of course, were all represented in certain mythological episodes with the features of a cat, witness to the great mysteries of creation.

The extreme fertility of the cat was considered as a divine sign, and women placed themselves under the protection of the cat-goddess Bast to have beautiful children. They also did what they could to make themselves as beautiful as the goddess's animal protector. Queen Cleopatra made up her eyes, elongating them as much as possible, to resemble her divine ancestor, Bast!

Femininity, felinity . . . In ancient Greece, Artemis, or Diana as she was known to the Romans, finding herself pursued, did not hesitate to change herself into a cat in order to escape a cruel fate.

This somewhat pagan link between the woman and the cat caused harm to both during the Middle Ages. Women, possessing the secret of many mysteries, were judged to be witches; cats, strange and incomprehensible, were also considered diabolical by nature.

The cat maintains its claws with a care equal to that of a woman who manicures and polishes her nails: one more similarity between the two!

Cats are excellent mothers, jealously guarding the well-being and safety of their kittens. When several cats raise a litter together, they may take turns nourishing the newborns, while one of them goes out to hunt for food.

With her period of sexual heat lasting several days, a cat can be impregnated by two males and give birth, several days apart, to two litters. Weaning takes place at the end of five or six weeks: The kitten already has its milk teeth.

The maternal relationship is primordial for the kitten: The mother makes it possible for her kitten to learn, in several weeks, the basics for survival.

In German and Scandinavian mythology, Freyja, the goddess of love, appears in a chariot drawn by four sumptuous white cats.

Independence

We typically contrast the obedience of the dog with the independence of the cat, without hesitating to promote the idea that the dog bonds with its master while the cat bonds with its home. This is far from being the case! This misunderstanding comes from the fact that the cat cannot be tamed, and that its "willfulness" works against it, to the point of making it, in the minds of some, eternally insubordinate. In reality, the cat enjoys human company. It is sufficiently "flexible" to accommodate the most diverse lifestyles, whether as pampered house cat in a city apartment or as valued mouser living out-of-doors in a rural setting. One study has shown that cats look for an emotional bond with humans even before food.

Even when it involves petting, the cat likes to decide for itself whether or not it wishes to sit in your lap. If you take the initiative, its stay will be shorter, just to let you know who is master!

?Games

Which of the two friends is having the most fun?

More playful than a kitten? There is no such thing! And the amazing thing, for the cat, is that it retains this enthusiasm for play throughout its life, a kind of corollary to hunting activity. By observing them, humans have invented games occasionally inspired by the behavior of their pets.

The most well-known game? Cat and mouse. Children hold hands and make a circle. The mouse is inside the circle, the cat prowls on the outside and tries to force its way in to "crush" the mouse, while the children sing: "Purr, purr, purr, naughty cat. What have you done with your mouse?"

If the cat succeeds in catching its prey, the latter takes its place. On the other hand, if the mouse escapes, it must continue around the circle of dancers while meowing! The game of cat and mouse can also be played by blindfolding the eyes of the two children playing the animals. Their companions sit on the ground, forming two lines, each group helping its champion with directions. Finally, there is a more "erotic" version! The cat, when it catches the mouse, must kiss it. Among the classic feline games, there is the cat and the rat—a somewhat sadistic amusement. There are two players, the cat and the rat, while the other children remain as spectators. Cat and rat, blindfolded, are each tied to one end of a rope, attached in the middle to a stake planted in the ground. The cat is armed with a kind of bat; the rat has only a wood saw, on which it plays an

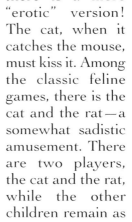

A simple string, perhaps with a cork attached: Why look for something more complicated in order to play?

For the cat, a stuffed animal can take the part of its prey: The hunter has not yet had the last word.

unpleasant "tune" in order to signal its location to the cat. And it must do so when the cat cries: "A rat! A rat!" The poor rodent must try to avoid the cat's blows. The massacre lasts for a time that has been agreed upon in advance. At the end, the two adversaries remove their blindfolds, the rat tends to its wounds, if need be, then two other children replace them.

It is not good to be either the cat or the mouse in these games, a reflection of the cruelty of the world of predators into which the children apparently have no difficulty entering with total inge-nuousness! In the same vein, another great classic is the game of "off-ground tag," which goes even further. Here, lots are drawn to determine who will be the cat, who must hunt down the others. They can escape only by jumping up on a chair or any other object that enables them to leave the ground. The one who is caught without having had the time to leap on a perch becomes the cat. Of course, seen from this point of view, this is merely a game designed to encourage speed and agility. But the devil that chooses the cat, or the ogre we might even say, is not innocent. This game recalls ancient customs capable of sending a chill down the spine since, as Roger Caillois quite seriously explains, it is a distant reminder of human sacrifice! "Beneath the innocence and childish roughness," he writes in *Games and Men*, "we recognize the frightful choice of a propitiatory victim: selected by destiny, before being selected by the nonsense syllables of the counting rhyme, the victim could [at least we suppose] get rid of its stain, passing it on by touch to the victim that it captures."

I play with this ball, but it is a bird that I see fluttering above my head. I never grow tired of this kind of game . . .

Play, for the cat, is also a continuous exercise in the coordination of its movements.

Dog

To get along "like cats and dogs" is never a good sign in matters of friendly or social relationships. What do they have in common, these two eternal antagonists of the animal kingdom? Very little, except for the fact that human beings have chosen both as companions. The dog accepts training that makes it, within its adoptive human family, the last of the pack. The cat, resistant to all commands, ignores this hierarchy, behaving like a conqueror, contrasting its independence with the obedience of the dog. The supposed rivalry between cat and dog dates back, perhaps, to the origins of domestication, with each of the two animals attempting to supplant the other within the heart of the family. A Walloon story recounts with humor that Saint Peter himself had established the rules for cohabitation, with dogs warming themselves by the fireplace during the day, and cats at night. Feline cunning quickly whittled away several daylight hours, and since then dogs have hated cats!

Weather

When a cat reaches its paw behind its ear, there will be rain. In many countries, "popular wisdom" accepts this as fact, despite the absence of scientific rigor. Is the cat, like the frog, an expert meteorologist?

In the fifteenth century, in the *Gospels of the Frog*, the chronicler had already noted: "When you see a cat sitting on a window in the sun, and the paw that it raises goes behind the ear, you can be sure that there will be rain the same day. . . ." In fact, this posture is part of its grooming behavior, the paw being the "washcloth" that reaches the top of the head!

In the past, in several religions, the cat was more or less consciously associated with the divinities responsible for bringing rain. In Egypt, the cat was considered an animal that brought fertility, as it was in China, Cambodia, and in India, where a caged cat was paraded through the streets of villages so that its meowing would move Indra and other divinities to send abundant rainfall to assure good harvests. Our ancestors saw omens in the various postures of the cat linked to changes in weather. If it purred while rubbing its muzzle, it was a sign of good weather. If it was agitated, scratching the ground and the carpet then climbing the curtains, storms and tempests were on the way. A nervous cat meant wind, with the cat scratching the ground in the direction from which the gusts would come. When an animal approached the fireplace, bad weather would arrive, especially when the tomcat showed its hindquarters to the hearth: a sure sign of a snowfall! It is true that the animal adopts a different position when sleeping, according to the temperature. In cold weather, the cat rolls up in a ball; the higher the mercury, the

In olden days, the cat was considered an animal as reliable as the frog in predicting weather.

more it stretches out to capture the coolness of the ground. Thus, it should come as no surprise that cats approach the chimney—or more prosaically the radiator—when the weather is cold!

Scientists are inclined to think that the cat is capable of sensing the onset of a storm, cyclone, tempest, earthquake, or volcanic eruption. A sixth sense? Without a clear understanding of the "receptors" that a cat possesses, we have often interpreted as a premonition the sensitivities a cat has developed as an organism adapted for survival in nature. The cat is sensitive to increases in static electricity, to rapid changes in the magnetic field, to increases in ground vibrations. Hence, it has the ability to sense before we do the imminent approach of certain meteorological phenomena or extremes of climate. Reliable accounts describe cats meowing feverishly to leave a house and run away, an earthquake occurring only minutes later. There are also stories of tomcats run-

ning for shelter while the sun is shining; moments later, storm clouds cover the sky and lightning flashes on the horizon.

We understand why fishermen have carefully observed the behavior of cats—to the point of traveling with them: On board, the cat enables them to avoid being caught in a squall, as its extreme nervousness is a sure sign of an approaching storm. Is the cat cleaning its face? There will be rough seas ahead. At the same time, a purring cat is a sign of calm waters. In our own time, weather forecasts broadcast on radio and television have replaced the generous advice of cats. But is this a valid reason not to observe them? Their predictions are sometimes as reliable as those of our specialists.

Fishermen who crossed paths with a cat while preparing to set sail preferred to stay in port; this was a sure sign of a storm.

Jumping

The cat is an expert in the art and technique of landing on its feet, with a dexterity and an elegance that continue to surprise us. If it is capable of acrobatics and of completing certain vertiginous leaps into the air from which it often escapes unscathed, it is thanks to the prophet Mohammed, at least according to an oriental legend first recounted in France in the seventeenth century by the botanist Tournefort. The father of Islam was preparing to go to prayer. He did not wish to disturb his cat Muezza, who was sleeping on the tail of his robe, and he preferred to tear the cloth rather than awaken her. Returning from the mosque, Mohammed was greeted with great affection by the little cat, who thanked him with her most graceful bow. The prophet passed his hand across her back three times and since that time, it is said, cats have always landed on their feet.

1

2

3

4

5

The reality is equally amazing. The internal ear of the cat can sense and control the speed that the body experiences when falling; this releases a gyroscopic reflex stimulating the semicircular canals: The cat completes a coordinated series of muscular flexions that enable it to turn around quickly and to return to a horizontal position before impact. The impact is often less serious when the cat falls from a great height: The resistance of the air in this case acts like a brake.

6

Grooming

The maternal example is basic for the inexperienced kitten.

After each meal, the cat always engages in a bit of grooming.

The cleanliness of the cat is legendary. Unlike the dog, the domestic cat does not need its owner's help to remain irreproachably clean. It should be said that a cat devotes 30 to 50 percent of its waking hours to this activity! Following the example of its mother, the kitten begins to lick itself after two weeks. After one month of life, it has already become a master of the art.

Its tools? Its tongue, which enables it to lick most of its body; its teeth, which are used to comb its fur and extract possible parasites; and the forepaws, which, damp with saliva, serve as a washcloth for the face, the top of the head, and the ears. In addition to its hygienic function, licking serves three important purposes: social (a means of communication), anxiolitic (stress reduction), and nutritive (the skin synthesizes vitamin D). The cleanliness of the cat is a sign of good health. If the cat neglects its grooming, a visit to the veterinarian is called for without delay.

The remedy for fleas is scratching: that's better!

With its tongue, the cat is able to directly clean a portion of its face.

The art of grooming: real choreography.

It is comforting to be able to help out a friend!

Sleep

The cat might have been called the sloth, if this name had not already been used by another small mammal that spends its entire days in the trees. Sixteen hours of sleep per day: What could be better? Insomnia, it's unheard of! An enlightened amateur, the cat divides its periods of sleep based on a diurnal and nocturnal rhythm, to better savor the delights of small, restorative naps! The cat spends the major part of its existence (70 percent) sleeping. It has the ability that some of us may envy: passing effortlessly from a sleeping state to a waking state, and vice versa. What can be more soothing than observing a cat preparing to sleep? Depending on the temperature and the season, the cat sleeps in a ball or stretched out, then falls into the first phase of light sleep. The muscular tone remains. Then the posture of the animal changes considerably: The muscles relax; the eyes move under the closed lids; the paws, the face, the whiskers move fit-

The cat is capable of taking a short nap wherever it finds itself, and its idea of comfort may not conform to our standards.

Even when it is in a deep sleep, the cat always sleeps with one ear open. In nature, it must be able to detect the approach of a predator.

fully; and the cat breathes more rapidly. This is deep sleep, when, paradoxically, the cat dreams. About what? About everything a cat does in its daily life: stalking, hunting, grooming, for example. Only erotic dreams are absent from feline dream activity!

The phases of light sleep (approximately 25 minutes) and of deep sleep (approximately five minutes) can alternate for several hours if the cat is not disturbed. A cat accustomed to living in an apartment and sleeping in our presence is totally capable of adapting its sleep pattern to ours and remaining asleep all night.

An older cat needs long periods of sleep to remain in good health.

We would love to know what our sleeping cat is dreaming about. Is it about us?

Behavior

When we adopt a cat, we considerably alter the way of life it would have had in the wild. However, certain important characteristics of its behavior remain. What are the basic activities of the cat? Hunting and playing, feeding, reproducing, grooming, and elimination, without forgetting sleep—a cat sleeps approximately 16 hours per day, which represents 70 percent of its existence. Hunting? This makes it possible for the cat, in the wild, to feed itself. In an apartment this activity is, of course, reduced. Flies replace more traditional prey such as rabbits, rodents, and birds! Nevertheless, certain games, by keeping the cat in good physical condition despite a sedentary life, provide an excellent alternative. Food? Contrary to what was long believed, the cat is a discriminating gourmet who appreciates a varied diet, guided above all by a sensitive sense of smell.

Although the cries characteristic of the cat in heat have wrongly given it a reputation of lubricity, the sexuality of the cat is geared toward a single purpose, reproduction. Females reach sexual maturity at around six to eight months, males between ten and twelve months. While the latter are always ready for action, it is not the same for the females, who only allow themselves to be approached during heat (which occurs at more or less brief intervals depending on the breed, the environment, etc.). Spaying and removal of the ovaries, often practiced to prevent unwanted litters, suppress in part the related behaviors (urinary marking, crying). The cleanliness of the cat is a quality that we particularly prize. Elimination behavior develops spontaneously at the age of one month along with grooming, which the kitten masters at the same time, and to which the cat devotes between 30 to 50 percent of its waking hours. The cat adapts very well to life in an apartment, to such an extent that it gives the impression of owning the place. Which is, in fact, the truth, since it ignores all hierarchy.

Attentive, all senses alert, ready for anything . . .

In scratching wood or cloth, the cat marks its territory and leaves its imprint: a word to the wise!

Perfectly integrated in the family unit.

The rules of feline precedence are very complicated.

The domestic tiger at leisure; the cat appreciates domestic comforts.

It's also good on the floor!

It is difficult to prevent the cat from doing everything we forbid dogs to do. A cruel dilemma for those who obey . . .

Selected Parts

Eyes

British Shorthair

Persian Colorpoint

Scottish Fold

A large part of the fascination of the cat is due to its look. The Egyptians noticed that the animal was capable of withstanding the brightness of the sun by contracting the pupil, the iris being nothing more than a slit, while, in the dark, it expands to become round like the moon. The cat's vision, somewhat blurry up close, is excellent from a distance, and its remarkable field of vision—180 degrees—makes it a stalker without equal, capable of seeing the approach of prey and predators with acuity. The cat sees in colors: It can distinguish green and blue, and more vaguely, red. This rather imperfect color vision is less important than its excellent black and white nocturnal vision, the result of a large number of rods covering the retina.

The green gleam of the cat's eye—red in the Siamese—in the dark is from the layer of pigments that covers the back of the retina. This reflective layer increases luminosity, making it possible for the cat to see better in shadows.

British Shorthair

The eye of the cat may be perfectly round or almond-shaped; each breed has a different look.

Birman

Domestic Cat

Domestic Cat

Japanese Bobtail

Singapura

Korat

Ocicat

British Shorthair

Ragdoll

Maine Coon

The cat's iris has a particularly powerful muscular system that makes it possible for the animal to contract or dilate the pupil at will, according to the degree of luminosity. In the Middle Ages, the "phosphorescent" brightness of the cat's eye in the shadows contributed to its reputation as a diabolical animal.

Devon Rex

Ears

A noise?
The cat can
move its ears
independently
of each other in
order to locate
the source.

In the British Shorthair, the
ears match its round face.

The cat could be a formidable music critic. Its auditory system, more developed than that of the dog and especially of man, captures high frequency sounds with surprising precision. The cat can detect the tenth of a tone in high frequencies. That means it is almost capable of correcting a soprano whose high notes are not exactly on key!

The cat can direct either of its ears in the direction of a sound it finds intriguing. It is perfectly capable of recognizing the voices of several people and of hearing the "conversation" of mice from a considerable distance.

No additional maintenance for
the ears of the Scottish Fold!

Real tents,
sensitive even
to ultrasound.

Without hair,
the ears of the
Sphinx are high,
broad, and widely spaced.
The color of the skin is
as visible here as it is on
the rest of the cat's body.

What does he hear? We
can't begin to imagine.

86

Whiskers

Nothing worth noting:
My whiskers are resting.

They are commonly known as "whiskers" but their scientific name is vibrissa. These hairs, which are found both at the level of the eyebrows and at the end of the forepaws, serve more than an aesthetic function. Of a thicker diameter than other hairs, extremely mobile, with receptors at their base, they are connected to the brain by the nervous system and provide the cat with much useful information. The vibrissa serve as antennas for the cat to use in finding its bearings in the world that surrounds it and to guide it in complete darkness. They make it possible for the cat to recognize the surfaces of objects or obstacles to be circumvented or avoided. In hunting, the vibrissa are equally important. Sensitive to shifts in the air and the smallest movement, they assist the cat in grasping its "game," as they are in contact with the prey even before the cat has seized it, indicating exactly where the teeth are to be planted. Never cut the whiskers of a cat!

What? Prey?
Let's quickly
straighten our
whiskers.

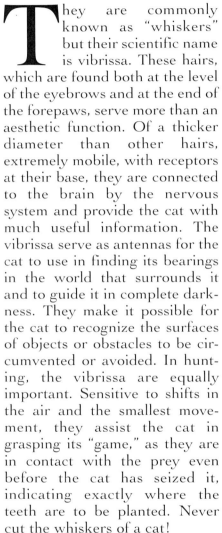

Let's explore the surroundings:
Whiskers extending in all directions
identify the smallest obstacle.

When someone tries to pick a
fight with me, I become a lion!

*Whiskers forward,
on alert . . .*

*Each set of whiskers is of a different
length: This is ideal for judging volume.*

$\mathcal{F}ur$

Turkish
Angora

Scottish Fold

Ocicat

What is softer and more pleasant to the touch than a cat's fur? Without wishing to anger the Sphinx, the naked cat whose skin (which is covered with a fine layer of down) is nevertheless warm and agreeable to the touch, the feline coat is one of the cat's most seductive traits.

Its color, its texture, its length often determine our choice of breed. The cat's coat consists of three different types of hair. The longest, which determines the principal color of the fur, is the topcoat; it covers the guard hairs, which are shorter and more fine; finally, the down, more present on the belly than on the back, covers the skin. The coat provides the cat with equal protection against cold and heat (the hair changes orientation according to the temperature), but also against the shocks and wounds that may be inflicted by claws or teeth. Every cat owner has noted that, when one pets a cat for a long time, its fur becomes charged with static electricity.

One of the major assets of feline beauty is the wide range of coats that the cat is capable of wearing.

Cornish Rex

Norwegian
Forest Cat

Exotic
Shorthair

Scottish
Fold

Norwegian
Forest Cat

Selkirk
Rex

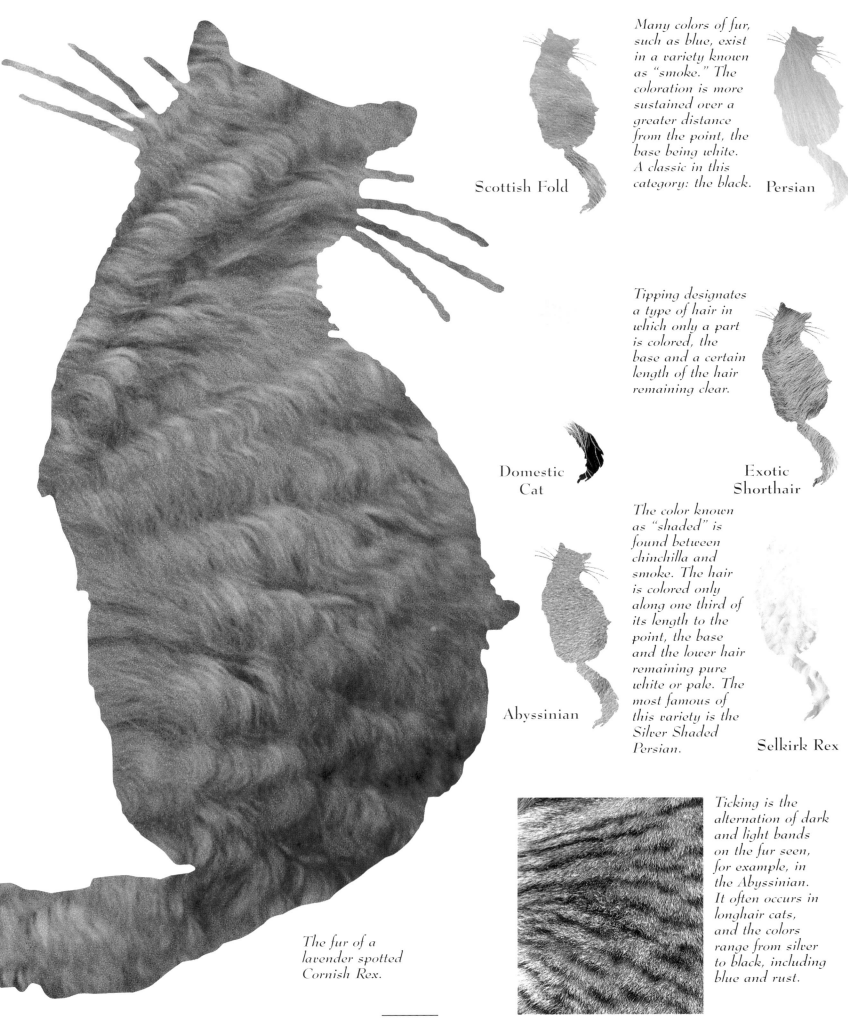

Many colors of fur, such as blue, exist in a variety known as "smoke." The coloration is more sustained over a greater distance from the point, the base being white. A classic in this category: the black.

Scottish Fold

Persian

Tipping designates a type of hair in which only a part is colored, the base and a certain length of the hair remaining clear.

Domestic Cat

Exotic Shorthair

The color known as "shaded" is found between chinchilla and smoke. The hair is colored only along one third of its length to the point, the base and the lower hair remaining pure white or pale. The most famous of this variety is the Silver Shaded Persian.

Abyssinian

Selkirk Rex

The fur of a lavender spotted Cornish Rex.

Ticking is the alternation of dark and light bands on the fur seen, for example, in the Abyssinian. It often occurs in longhair cats, and the colors range from silver to black, including blue and rust.

Claws

With claws and teeth, the cat has incredible dexterity.

All claws bared, the cat plays without effort in the feline court, in which it has—in a minor key—the power to attack. Claws make it possible for the cat to demonstrate its talents as a climber. Formidable instruments for seizing its prey and defending itself, they are also a tool for marking the territory where it lives, whether the trunks of trees in the garden or the cushions in an apartment.

Clawing also prevents the claws from becoming too long. The ends of claws can be trimmed, but their removal is strictly discouraged: The cat, thus mutilated, loses its means of defense and part of its dexterity. Never forget that under each claw sleeps a velvet paw and that a happy cat is more likely to hide this weapon from us, reserving it for its enemies.

Velvet paws, as long as the need to jump does not present itself.

Some cats truly give the impression of having small hands. Their claws make it possible for them to grasp and hold prey, toys, or food.

Tail

Tail in the shape of a question mark to welcome its master.

Lewis Carroll's *Alice's Adventures in Wonderland* may have immortalized the popular simile, "grinning like a Cheshire cat," but the most expressive part of the cat is really its tail. The cat's tail, necessary for balance, also enables it to communicate with other cats and with us. It is therefore desirable to know how to decode this unique language. The cat that is coming toward us—or toward another cat—with its tail raised, the tip a bit curved, is friendly and welcoming. A tail between the legs is a sign of fear; raised and inflated, the hairs standing out, it expresses anger or surprise. It should be noted that a repetitive movement of the tail calls for the greatest caution: This indicates that the animal is annoyed.

I am approaching with curiosity . . .

In presenting its genital-anal zone, tail lifted, this small female assumes in front of the male the posture that she observed when she was a kitten, face to face with her mother.

Hunger? Excitement? The tail is folded across the back.

In activities that are playful or athletic, the tail maintains an up-raised position.

Cat Beauty and the Champion Cat

Although the cat is a clean animal, nothing prevents you from turning it into a little beauty, especially if it is a longhair cat. And if your kitty or your tom is a budding star that you intend to show in competition, grooming is required. A cat is either beautiful or it is not!

A cat used to grooming accepts in principle the restrictions of brushing.

It is difficult to be a star.

For cat fanciers and breeders, cat shows are the occasion to show the public the most beautiful specimens of each breed. It was in London that the first of these great cat shows took place in 1871, on the initiative of Harrison Weir. In France, the Cat Club was responsible for the first show, in Paris, in 1925. In America, the first official cat show was held in New York in 1895.

To participate in a cat show, you must be a member of a club or association. The cat must be in good health, have a pedigree, and be registered with the club to which it belongs.

It is important to prepare your cat for the event, physically, first of all, with health and grooming care required (worming, vitamins for the fur, bathing, daily brushing); and psychologically: The cat must be docile, calm, and not afraid to be handled by strangers. It must be able to charm the judges with its attributes and its composure. Perhaps you are the owner of a future champion, or even a "Supreme," the greatest prize that a cat can win at a show.

During the months that precede the show, you must regularly attend to grooming your cat. Five days before the big day, you must give it a bath so that it can show off its beautiful assets to the best advantage.

Who dares to say that cats do not like water?

One must patiently tolerate some discomfort in order to appear at one's best.

Untangling and smoothing the fur with a brush is an art in itself.

The great moment has arrived, for the cat . . . and especially for its masters: Receiving a prize at a cat show is confirmation of the beauty of one's protégé.

Have You Seen — the Cat?

The Cat in Painting

The Egyptians were perhaps the first to fix the image of the cat, in the tomb frescoes of the Theban necropolis, more than 4,000 years ago. Our friend the cat would then have to be very patient: Its bad reputation, during the Middle Ages, prolonged its absence from the artist's studio and palette. But what a spectacular return! Beginning in the fifteenth century, the cat made its appearance in Italian Renaissance paintings, where it was portrayed in numerous religious scenes. The France of Louis XV welcomed it in turn. Flemish and British artists made it a charming presence in family scenes. The Romantics and Impressionists gave it a more important role, while it became, for the Japanese—Hokusai, Hiroshige—a minor household god or a demon. Modern artists continued to appreciate the cat: Matisse, Miró, Chagall, Klee, Picasso, Balthus, R. P. Thrall, Edward Penfield, Paul Davis, Leonor Fini were all inspired by the charm, the mystery, the equivocal and incomparable physical beauty of the cat.

In this study of tigers and cats, Géricault (1791–1824) emphasizes the wild side of the domestic cat. The line drawing does justice to the exceptional physical beauty of two cats, which has inspired many artists throughout history.

Usually associated with women by the Impressionist painters, the cat here is the affectionate companion of the Boy with Cat *by Auguste Renoir (1841–1919).*

Pablo Picasso (1881–1973) particularly enjoyed the company of cats. He produced this impressive Cat Seizing a Bird (1939, © Succession Picasso 1998) in several versions, as he confided, "The subject obsessed me, I don't know why."

The White Cat by Théodore Géricault illustrates the peaceful and familiar aspect of the domestic cat. Lotto, Véronèse, Pontormo, Bruegel, Rembrandt, Fragonard, Chardin, Velázquez, Goya, Courbet, Manet, Gauguin, all used the cat as a model.

A *S*torybook
Cat

LE MAISTRE CHAT,

OU

LE CHAT BOTTE'.

CONTE.

VN Meuſnier ne
laiſſa pour tout
biens à tròis en-
fans qu'il avoit, que ſon

The painter and engraver Gustave Doré (1832–1883), inspired by Perrault, has given us the most successful and most well-known illustration of Puss-in-Boots.

An outlaw cat! Hungarian illustration by K. Savely Dezso.

For posterity, *Puss-in-Boots* or *The Master Cat*, one of the jewels in Charles Perrault's *Mother Goose Stories* (1697), remains the basic text.

It was in Venice that *Puss-in-Boots* made its first written appearance; Venice, a city built on the water, swarming with rats and mice, where the value of maintaining a large population of street cats was quickly understood. In 1550, Giovanni Straparola published in the city of the Doges a collection of stories entitled *The Mischievous Nights*, in which the famous cat (here a female) appeared, and the work was so successful that it was translated into French. From Venice, the inspiration traveled to Naples, where Giambattista Basile, also the author of *The Cinderella Cat*, featured *Puss-in-Boots* in one of the stories in his *Tale of Tales* (1634). Charles Perrault, who had certainly read Straparola and Basile, had an embarrassment of riches to choose from in creating his new version of the tale. *Mother Goose Stories* was an immediate and lasting success. The Brothers Grimm adapted *Puss-in-Boots* in the German language, while Tchaikovsky created, in his ballet *The Sleeping Beauty*, a pas de deux entitled "Puss-in-Boots and the White Cat." A surprising destiny, said some angry minds, for a cat that gave lessons in lying, theft, cruelty and cheating. The logic of the fable had little to do with traditional morality. As for *Puss-in-Boots*, Perrault had written his story at a time in which cats still did not enjoy the best of reputations. Perrault showed himself to be ahead of his time when he created the miller's son and his only "treasure," a simple cat. An elegant, subtle, and astute way of indicating to a seventeenth century audience the advantage of having a cat under one's roof: a useful animal, but also a daily companion, mischievous, comical, affectionate, capable of bringing sunshine by its tricks and mimicry into the saddest of lives.

The mischievous Puss-in-Boots has become the best friend and accomplice of children.

In my house I want
A sane woman
A cat among the books
Friends all year round
Without whom I cannot live.

Guillaume Apollinaire,
"The Cat," *The Bestiary
or Procession of Orpheus*

It is the familiar spirit of the place;
It judges, it presides, it inspires
Everything in its empire;
Perhaps it is a fairy, a god?

Charles Baudelaire,
"The Cat," *The Flowers of Evil*

She was playing with her cat
And it was a marvel to behold
The white hand and the white paw
Playing in the evening shadow.

Paul Verlaine,
"Woman and Cat,"
Saturnine Poems

The Poet's Cat

For poets, the cat is a muse, an inspiration, a silent and attentive witness to the pen scratching across the paper, a mysterious and intimate companion. This wandering animal, doesn't it resemble the poet, who searches for the images and the words that will convey a message? While La Fontaine showed no tenderness toward an animal that he disliked, most poets have celebrated the qualities and virtues of the cat.

As soon as he was within range, he saw the contestants,
Grippeminaud, the good apostle,
Scratching both sides,
Forcing the parties to agree by crushing one against another.

Jean de La Fontaine,
"The Cat, the Weasel and the Little Rabbit," *Fables,* book VII.

My heart is breaking
When I speak about him or I write:
It's Belaud, my little gray cat
Belaud who was by chance
The most beautiful work that nature
Created as far as cats are concerned.

Joachim Du Bellay
"Epitaph for a Cat," *Various Rustic Games*

Their fertile kidneys are full of magical sparks
And pieces of gold, along with a fine sand,
Their mystical eyes vaguely shining.

Charles Buadelaire,
"The Cats," *The Flowers of Evil*

Steinlen
the Art of the Cat

Théophile Alexandre Steinlen (1859–1923) is surely one of the artists who has contributed immensely to popularizing the image of the domestic cat thanks to his lithographed posters and his etchings. This Swiss artist, who made his career in Paris, knew better than anyone how to illustrate the various aspects of the cat: companion, children's friend, artist's inspiration, and symbol of independence.

Living in Montmartre, Steinlen had ample opportunity to mix with the cats that would make his reputation. It was at the foot of the Butte Montmartre, in 1881, that the celebrated cabaret *The Black Cat* opened under the direction of Rodolphe Salis. Frequented by the best artists and poets, this unique spot did much for Steinlen's reputation; the poster he created in 1896 for the *Black Cat* tour is one of his best known. Steinlen's view of cats, both realistic and sentimental, is rooted in the social context of his time, which gives his work its expressive force.

Created in 1894, this poster shows Colette, Steinlen's daughter (who reappears in Des Chats)*, along with the family's three cats.*

This Steinlen lithograph toured the world, uniquely symbolizing the Montmartre spirit and the irrepressible spirit of the cat. It was an incomparable success.

In 1898, Steinlen devoted 26 engravings to his cats and those from his neighborhood.

The Celebrity's Cat

Many famous people have loved their cats—to such an extent that the fame of some of these exceptional cats has been handed down to posterity, like that of their mistresses and masters. From the cats of Mark Twain and Ernest Hemingway; Charles Dickens's cat Williamina; the cats of Colette, Céline, and Cocteau; Abraham Lincoln's son's pet, Tabby, who may have been the first First Cat; and Bill Clinton's black and white domestic cat, Socks—the list of celebrity cats is long. "In spending time with cats," wrote Colette in *The Tendrils of the Vine*, "we only become richer." Between novelist and cat, this relationship of love and mutual esteem has never failed.

The Cat
in Advertising

Advertising was still new, and already the cat had played a role! In 1868, Édouard Manet gave the cat its letters of nobility by drawing the poster used to promote the book written by his friend Champfleury, *The Cats*. Other major artists such as Toulouse-Lautrec and Steinlen used the cat as a model, in order to promote the charm of an actress, the interest of a show, the quality of a brand of milk or of chocolate.

From toothpaste to cigarette paper, from chocolate to mustard, from jewels to beauty products, not to mention a brand of wool or that of heating appliances, the cat is the advertiser's best friend. This could be because cats had come to play an intimate role in our daily lives and they projected an image of refinement and seduction. Cats were even used to "sell" depilatory cream, something their oldest rival, the dog, could never have done!

felix 🐾

Felix, a likeable cat used in advertisements for French cat food.

Don't touch my whiskers! An amazing poster from 1925.

Even a cat could write with a pen! Poster by Lochard (c. 1910).

Our friend the cat helps to sell shoes, in an old American advertising poster.

Does the cat like to smoke? We may wonder, but this poster by Belimbau (c. 1910) was a great success.

The poster artist Henry Gerbault (1868–1930) seemed unaware in 1895 that chocolate is poisonous for cats as well as for dogs.

Appearing on the market in France recently, the Felix brand of cat food found an irresistible ally in its black and white cat. Amusing and unaffected, Felix is a domestic cat with whom we can easily identify our own cats.

The Cat
in Movies

If there is an animal capable of stealing the limelight from the biggest stars, it is certainly the cat. It is natural that such a charmer should seduce screenwriters and directors, to such an extent that it would be difficult to list all of the numerous appearances of the cat on the screen. Mephistophelian companion of the "evil" Donald Pleasance in the James Bond film *You Only Live Twice*, alone in space with Sigourney Weaver to fight against the *Alien*, joyous character in Walt Disney's *Aristocats*, always ready for a chase in *Tom and Jerry*, the cat on the screen—real or cartoon character—brilliantly shows us the various aspects of its personality.

The Cat *(1967): the hellish life of a couple, as seen by Georges Simenon. Between Simone Signoret and Jean Gabin, the cat is an emotional prize whose murder precipitates the drama.*

Breakfast at Tiffany's *(1961): Audrey Hepburn, a zany New Yorker, adopts Cat, an alley cat of sturdy character, as bohemian as its mistress.*

Hateful, ferocious, and sexy: three qualifications required for Catwoman (here, Michelle Pfeiffer in Batman Returns, *1992).*

Bell, Book and Candle
(1958): Kim Novak, a
modern-day witch, seduces
James Stewart with the
help of a Siamese cat,
Pyewacket, who makes
the unhappy suitor sneeze
every time it appears.

Beauty and the Beast *(1945): Jean Cocteau was inspired by
the face of a Persian Blue cat to create the extraordinary mask
of the beast worn by Jean Marais.*

A charming
Hollywood
anachronism: In
The Egyptian
(1954), Bella
Darvi (here with
Edmund Purdom)
owns a ravishing
white Persian . . .
unknown in the
Egypt of the
Pharaohs.

The Cat as Object

I nside every cat lover is a collector of objects. And there are many that celebrate their animal of choice! All it takes is a cat figurine, received as a birthday or holiday gift, and the addiction takes root. As the world of cat objects is enormous and continually growing, the joys of discovery will never be exhausted.

The ancient Egyptians had already crafted wooden toys in the shape of cats. But the real fashion for cat objects dates to the last century, especially for bronzes. Today, the passion for cats continues to inspire creative fantasy. Whether as collectibles or utilitarian objects, kitsch or comical figurines, cats are an inexhaustible subject for which young and old alike willingly break open their piggy banks (in the form of a cat, of course)!

Musical mechanical toy: a romantic scene between male and female cats.

Porcelain perfume bottle (China).

Cat carved out of buffalo horn (Thailand).

A mechanical toy in tinware: A winding mechanism makes it possible to activate the tail.

A cat and her kittens in porcelain.

Children's table in painted wood in the shape of a cat (Philippines).

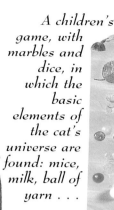

Mailbox in varnished wood from the early twentieth century.

A children's game, with marbles and dice, in which the basic elements of the cat's universe are found: mice, milk, ball of yarn . . .

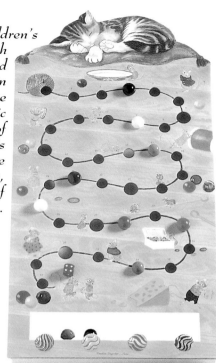

Bronze ashtray (replica of a model from the previous century). The infernal duo, "cat and fish," is once more the subject.

Statuette in painted wood in the Latin American style.

Bottle of red wine from Chile, Gato Negro ("black cat"). In addition to its quality, this wine comes with a little black plastic cat.

Very beautiful porcelain cats with glass eyes (Great Britain).

The Cat
in Postcards

Today we prefer photographs, and there are beautiful ones, often in color or in black and white by well-known photographers, celebrating the beauty of the cat or the comic nature of its poses. But for a long time, beginning in the late nineteenth century, picture postcards of the cat were all the rage, and those showing cats are now quite sought after by collectors.

Most of the time there were standard scenes, funny, original, or moving, showing cats in situations that were more human than animal!

Some of the authors of these feline cards have remained anonymous, but others, such as the Briton Louis Wain and the German Arthur Thiele, created feline silhouettes of great charm, with real characters whose pranks were followed from card to card. These are collectibles today, and their value can easily make their owners purr with contentment.

AU BON MARCHÉ

Great favorites since the early days of postcards, kittens are capable of softening even the hardest heart! Who could resist a message brought by these small marvels?

The Cat
in Postage Stamps

What could be nicer when sending mail than to entrust it to that ideal messenger, the cat? Many countries throughout the world have paid tribute, in various ways, to the cat. Representations of various breeds are the most popular, followed by groups of kittens. Characters from comic strips and well-known tales, such as *Puss-in-Boots*, are also favored by the postal services. France remains a poor relation in the area of feline philately, which is somewhat surprising in a country with a population of approximately eight million domestic cats.

The Cat
in Calendars

A calendar selection would be incomplete without the cat. And what more perfect Christmas gift could there be to grace the walls of a cat lover's kitchen than color photographs of Cats and Kittens, Cats in Art, Country Cats, Cartoon Cats, Garfield, or Felix the Cat, among others? Cat protection societies, as well as proponents of many major cat breeds, use desk and wall calendars, filled with cat-care tips and tidbits, to promote their ideals, while electronic calendars with cat screensavers have become desktop mainstays for feline-loving computer users.

Beliefs and Superstitions

Sorcery and the Black Cat

I f one cat has excited passions and continues to do so, it is the black cat. Even now, there are still sad characters who will tell you that crossing the path of a black cat brings bad luck, especially if it comes from the left. But cat fanciers will happily tell you that nothing is more beautiful and more fascinating than a black cat, an astonishing turnaround for an animal that had the sad privilege, for centuries, of symbolizing the evil powers of darkness when it was not taken for the devil incarnate. The Church, under Pope Gregory IX, did not hesitate to solemnly condemn the cat in 1233: The Papal bull, *Vox in rama* denounced the devil that was hidden in every black cat and, for the same reason, anyone who owned one of these diabolical animals. Throughout the Christian West, where the black cat, preferred companion of witches, had already established a bad reputation, it was the signal for a massacre. Burned, hanged, stoned, the black cat was mercilessly put to death. Only a tuft of white hair on the chest—called the "finger of God" or "mark of the angel"—redeemed the cat in the eyes of its torturers. Why such murderous fury? It was probably due to the fact that the color black, the color of mourning and shadows, took on a more evil connotation during the Middle Ages: It was the color of the devil. And the black coat of the cat, isn't it a sacrilegious imitation of the priest's black cassock? The black cat was blamed for all of the world's evils. The fear of the black cat, among our ancestors, was equivocal: This animal, so disturbing, was also thought to bring good luck.

Burned, hanged, or stoned, the black cat was mercilessly put to death.

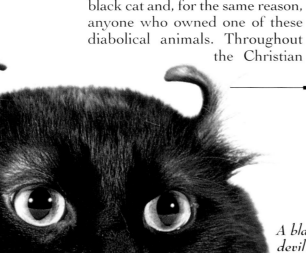

A black devil? No, simply an American Curl on the defensive.

Enough to impress the superstitious . . .

If the black cat was part of the "witch's kitchen," it was also unfortunately called the "rabbit of the poor."

How could such a beautiful animal be the cause of so many massacres throughout history?

"It is true that the color black caused much harm to the cat's reputation in the popular imagination: it made the fire in their eyes flame even more, which is enough to make many believe that they were at least sorcerers." Moncrif, Cats (1727).

In Provence and in Brittany, if you signed a pact with the devil, the black cats that slept close to the hearth were forced to leave in search of gold during the night. But the cat would have to be sold to avoid losing one's soul . . .

Proverbs

Many expressions that we use were formulated by our ancestors based on observations of daily life. An example? "The cat likes fish but it hates to get its paws wet." The language of business and commerce has also known how to use the cat. For example, the old saying, "To pay in cats and dogs," means to pay, not in cash, but in inconvenient commodities.

When it comes to food, the cat is always ready to steal and to scrounge! The old French proverb, "The cat often makes off with the tastiest morsel," has its equivalents in Great Britain, Germany, and Italy. For the French and the Germans, "The cat is hungry when it eats bread." And the latter, like the Italians, are on their guard when they say: "Don't trust the roast to the cat that licks the skewer."

Hypocrite? Did you say hypocrite? Our stalking tomcat, who pretends to be sleeping, is a bit of a coaxer, or *gatta morta* ("dead cat") in Italian and *tote Katze* in German. Italians have their own expression when their prey escapes them and they wish to show disdain: "When the cat cannot reach the bacon, it says that it is rancid"!

And sensuality—in France, it is well known that a woman in love is "in love like a cat."

Sometimes a cat is lost during a linguistic voyage. Thus in Britain "A cat can look a king in the face," and in France, "A dog can look a bishop in the face"!

When it rains "cats and dogs" better take shelter at once. If you are able to quickly turn around a situation, it is said that you know how to "flip the cat in the frying pan." And it is to the British that we owe the invention of the sinister "cat-o'-nine-tails," since it is from the English that we get this marvelous saying about the animal's lack of unselfishness: "The cat doesn't trap mice for God."

"A cat has nine lives."

"When the cat's away the mice will play."

"Curiosity killed the cat."

"At night,

"The cat's out of the bag."

"To fight like cats and dogs."

"A good cat deserves a good rat."

"There's more than one way to skin a cat."

"He who plays with cats must expect to get scratched."

"To look like the cat that swallowed the canary."

"All things belong to cats, in a cat's eye."

all cats are gray."

"You got the wrong cat by the tail that time."

The Nine Lives
of the Cat

Of all the animals that surround us, the cat is perhaps the one that most profoundly stimulated the imagination of our ancestors, to the point of giving rise to a number of amazing beliefs and superstitions, and also the idea of strange powers. It is claimed that cats have seven or nine lives, and are thus capable of defying death, to be reincarnated several times over. This association with the supernatural is surely the reason why cats have, at various times, been blamed for both bad and good luck. But for the providence of nature to bless cats with nine lives instead of one means they must possess some divine protection. What a charming belief for those who love cats. But, in the medieval context, where the animal was not considered saintly, we may wonder how this belief became widespread. It is probably due to the fact that the cat can, with astonishing energy, withstand depri-vation, illness, and bad treatment; and also perhaps because nothing so resembles a cat as another cat. At a time when they were killed without mercy, perhaps it was necessary to believe that a dead cat had returned when, in fact, it was another cat, hence, the ambiguity that gave rise to this legend. The British, during the eighteenth century, gave the nine lives of the cat a less poetic meaning: They gave the name "cat-o'-nine-tails" to a whip especially designed to punish sailors!

The mystery of the nine lives of the cat may come to us from ancient Egypt, whose mythology tells us that the first god, Atoum-Ra, carried within him the seed of eight other great gods in the Egyptian pantheon. If we are aware that the god Atoum was compared to a cat in the sacred text, the mystery becomes clear.

Accustomed to disappearing and reappearing after many days of absence from its home, the cat encouraged our ancestors to believe it had nine lives. (Miniature from the Book of Properties of Things, by Barthélemy de Glandville)

The Cat
in Astrology

The Egyptians believed the cat had been born in the constellation of the Lion. The domestic cat had less luck with western astronomers, and only Joseph Jérôme Lefrançois de Lalande (1732–1807) dared to add a cat consisting of 50 stars to the map of the heavens, at the end of the eighteenth century. Alas, it did not remain there for long: Camille Flammarion, who probably did not like cats, removed them less than 100 years later.

All that remained was for the cat to cling to its position in the Chinese zodiac as a way of justifying its authority in the realm of astrology. We must note in passing a slight problem of usurpation of identity: In China, the fourth sign, our Cancer, is not a cat but a hare. In the darkness, the leaps and long ears of the two animals can be confused and both are in harmony with the nocturnal and lunar symbolism, but this is stretching things. The Vietnamese, for their part, have opted for the cat, giving rise to this confusion and this assimilation between the two zodiacs, confirmed in our latitudes by the numerous admirers of the cat. Thus persons born in 1903, 1915, 1927, 1939, 1951, 1963, 1975, 1987, and 1999 are born in the Year of the Cat.

Some western astrologers think that our pets are influenced by the planets, like we are, and that it is possible to draw up a cat's astrological chart if the place, date, and time of birth are known. It is to be hoped that the cat's astrological profile is compatible with our own—otherwise life together will be hell!

The popularity of the cat has not ceased to grow and to be embellished, the animal having finally found its place in the bestiary of the Chinese zodiac.

Superstitions

In America, a white cat . . .

. . . is viewed as a symbol of good luck.

The people of Provence . . .

. . . believe that seeing cats play in the morning is the sign of a wasted day.

In Germany, if a black cat . . .

. . . was seen sleeping on a tomb, it was a sign that the devil had taken the soul of the deceased.

A Cat . . .

. . . onboard a ship is considered to bring luck.

In America, an old wives' tale . . .

. . . admonishes young mothers to keep cats away from babies, because a cat may "suck the breath" from an infant and suffocate it, presumably while trying to lick milk from the baby's mouth.

In Brittany,

fishermen crossing paths with a cat prior to sailing could expect a poor catch or a storm.

A young woman

who steps on the tail of a cat is doomed not to find a husband for a long time. The number of meows emitted by the cat is the number of years she will have to wait.

In America,

a black cat crossing one's path is perceived as a sign of bad luck. Another version of this superstition states that if a black cat walks toward you, it brings good fortune, but if it walks away, it takes the good luck with it.

A dying cat . . .

. . . in a house foretells the death of one of the people living under the same roof.

Cats born in May were bad.

Giving someone a cat was the best way to anger them.

O riginating in rural surroundings, many superstitions related to the cat indicate to what extent this familiar predator was considered as an animal distinct from other domestic animals. These superstitions were related first to experiences with cats encountered in daily life, then to speech, to certain trades, and finally to death.

Table of Contents

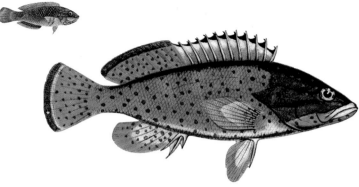

Bibliography

BRADSHAW John, *The Behaviour of the Domestic Cat*, C.A.B.
COPPÉ Philippe, *Les Chats en 1 000 Photos*, Solar
GAGNON Anne-Claire, CHAURAND Jean-Paul, LARUE Jean-François,
Comportement du chat et ses troubles, Le Point vétérinaire.
LAROCHE Robert de, *Histoire secrète du chat*, La Renaissance du livre.
LAROCHE Robert de, LE PAPE Gilles, *L'ABCdaire du chat*, Flammarion.
MONTRY Annie de, LEPEUVE Françoise, *Chat Pub*, Aubier.
MORRIS Desmond, *Le Chat révélé*, Calmann-Lévy.
MORRIS Desmond, *Parlons chat*, Calmann-Lévy.
ROUSSELET-BLANC Dr. Pierre, *Le Chat*, "Encyclopédie active," Larousse.
SACASE Christiane, *Les Chats*, "Guide Vert," Solar.
SÉBILLOT Paul, *Le Folklore de France*, Image.
WRIGHT Michael and WALTERS Sally, *Le Livre du chat*, Arted.

Photograph Credits

All of the photographs in this book are by Yves Lanceau except for:

p. 8 (top left and right): RMN/M. Chuzeville; p. 8 (bottom), p. 9 (left); Hervé Lewandowski/RMN; p. 16/17 (background photo): RMN/Jean; p. 102 (right): RMN; p. 102 (left): RMN/J.-G. Berizzi, p. 103 (top): RMN/J.-G. Berizzi © Succession Picasso 1998;

p. 9 (bottom center): Jean Guichard;
p. 11, p. 105 (top right and center right), p. 108, p. 109, p. 115 (top right), p. 135, p. 139: Jean-Loup Charmet;

p. 15 (bottom), p. 107 (top left and bottom right): Stefano Salviati;

p. 15 (top and center), pp. 12/13, p. 16, p. 17 (top right, bottom center), p. 41 (3rd photo from top), pp. 46/47 (background photo), p. 53 (top left), p. 60 (right and background photo), p. 66 (center), p. 103 (bottom right), p. 104 (large photo), p. 105 (top left), pp. 112/113, p. 122 (center right), p. 131 (bottom right), pp. 140/141: Roger-Viollet;

p. 27 (center right), p. 30 (Top right), p. 74 and p. 75: Jean-Marc Labat and Yves Lanceau;

p. 81 (top and bottom left), pp. 128/129: Michel Maïofiss;

p. 118/119: Michel Denancé and Michel Viard;

p. 106/107: Hervé Tardy;

p. 106 (top right and bottom right) and p. 107 (top right): Christophe L.;

p. 124 (top left) and p. 125 (bottom center): Spillers Petfood;

p. 126/127: Matthieu Prier;

pp. 136/137: Colette Portal;

p. 10, pp. 48/49, p. 64/65, p. 116 (bottom left), pp. 122/123 (background photo), p. 122 (top left), p. 123 (top photos), p. 131 (top right): D.R.

Acknowledgments

The photographer Yves Lanceau wishes to warmly thank all of the cats who so willingly posed, the amateur and professional breeders and most particularly the magazine Atout-Chat, Simon, Louis along with as Mitou and Miti, Thibault's lovely cats; without forgetting his dear colleague Isabelle Masson-Deblaize.

Fabienne Pavia and Sophie Greloux wishes to particularly thank Michel Denancé; Catherine Feuillie; Clémence and Valérie Greloux; Thérèse Guichard; Jean-Jacques and Laurence Hazan; Bruno and Marion Jillier; Michel Viard, Spillers Petfood; Éliane Stevens; the shop "Au chat dormant" for the loan of their objects; and the cats Cajou, Minette, Aphrodite and Grisbi.

English translation by Annie Heminway.
Contributing editor for English translation, Karen Leigh Davis.

Conceived and produced by Copyright for Éditions Solar
Graphic design: Ute-Charlotte Hettler
Layout: Odile Delaporte
Editorial design: Fabienne Pavia
Editorial coordination: Sophie Greloux and Fabienne Pavia

(cattus)